Hannah M. Teasdale was born a~ ̄
she was occasionally just
writing and competitive spc
others, pleasure and pain in ι

Hannah graduated from the L   ι798 and
then qualified as a Secondary Sc.   . ιe only vocation
that ever stuck, though, was writi.   ـ. first poetry collection,
Fingerprints was published in 2013 by Poetry Space.

Hannah has had plays produced for theatre and radio and
numerous short stories published in literary magazines. She
performs her poetry the length and breadth of the UK and can
be found in the spoken word tents at major festivals.

Hannah will forever love poetry and competitive sport but is
working hard on not breaking any more hearts – or bones.

Laid Bare

Hannah Teasdale

Burning Eye

This edition published by Burning Eye Books 2016

www.burningeye.co.uk
@burningeyebooks

Burning Eye Books
15 West Hill, Portishead, BS20 6LG

ISBN 978-1-909-136-77-9

Laid Bare

Lisa,

thank you for listening

x

CONTENTS

For John

BEST INTENTIONS

Your explanation for the letter, the one
you wrote in those hazy days
so long ago when
believing you could write wrongs better –
it didn't matter, you didn't grasp
I was too young to understand
the 'deeper connection' that was on offer
and as you found pleasure
in my cold hands, we both learnt
that I was never meant to be
your lover.
I didn't want to be caressed
by a more mature 'gentle touch'
but to lie across your kitchen table
and suck your joint after
I'd been fucked.
I didn't want to hear you say you love me –
but preferred to watch you consume
my sugared lies in bitesize pieces.
You have no reason to say
you're sorry.
It wasn't me whose heart grew lonely.
It isn't me whose tears won't dry.

1992

Remember us as kids?
Being told about spiders –
how in our sleep
they crawled across our faces
laying their eggs in our ears?
Or was it our mouths,
and we would eat them?

Either way, it freaked me out.

And how if you looked
in the mirror
at exactly midnight
Satan would stand behind
trying to stuff his cock in?
(Though I have a suspicion
this may just have been me.)

And those plastic bags
tied in trees'
branches full of witches' spells
waiting to cascade
over me?
And don't mention the sight
of a single, male crow –
that was definitely a lie
pushed towards me
by a treacherous hand
on the Ouija board.
And so was my guardian
angel, who *told* me
the hottest guy
in our class
would never fancy me.

What about those dawn skies –
still messed on acid;
the plastic bags morphing

into guilty faces?
Your boyfriend's face
reminding you of
someone else's?

Your own fingers –
filthy worms
out of touch
in sterile places.
Choking on dinner
with your stepdad
predicting the weather
whilst Mother?
Mother has a breakdown,
calls you *bitch*
as a jar of Hellman's
strikes your head?

Never since
have you even dared to open
the *lighter* version
mayonnaise.
And you can't keep a lover or
know what it means to be faithful –
you take it anywhere
wherever you can get it.
Anything to make others realise
you're still alive.

And you broke hearts
so many times –
and souls.
Tore families apart
but you couldn't know...
It was still beating although
you were dead inside

To all those you fucked with,
you just want to say,

Forgive me.
Let's make tomorrow
our brand new day.

The spiders haven't disappeared
but I don't mind
them crawling in my ears...

Plastic bags still blow in trees
but perhaps only holding secrets.
And Satan, years ago,
got sick
of my needy insecurity.

My husband's face
only ever looks better.
And Mum? Mum's on an even keel.
My stepdad will always love
discussing the weather.

PRIVATE COMMUNISM

It was around nine, that first desire
to take things that weren't mine
Not from real people,
those who counted.
I'd never take more
than I was owed.

No, wait!
That's a lie. I was nearer seven –
within a year of Mum leaving,
I'd built a collection,
eclectic items:
incense holders from
Pottery and Pieces, magazines
from the newsagent – full of tits and cunts
(fuck knows how I even reached them),
multi-packs of Heinz baked beans,
shoelaces wrapped in plastic,
Wrigley's spearmint gum
'on offer'. Stored
in shoeboxes under
our filthy bed. Untouched

until guilt ravaged me
through the night – the only way
to straighten my head,
to put things back
in different places.
Going round in Mummy's shadow
placing joss sticks back
between cheese slices
in Tesco. Handing out
penny chews to fellow Gnomes
at Brownies
(the Oxfam charity collection –
I'd already helped myself to).

All I ever kept
was a pack of Polos –

habitually inspected, curled
around my little fingers,
sniffed, licked.

I had some Tic Tacs too
to pop when things got bad –
like Mum would.
But it never stopped...
By thirteen, I had reams of knickers,
M&S bras I could never fill.
The high street making it
far too easy.
Saturday's favourite, the jelly bean stand
at BHS. Weren't even stealing
if you could linger
between the aisles and eat them.

A black silk shirt, size ten
(in the days when that
represented the average population),
was my downfall.
A life-long ban from C&A,
a fitting punishment
for the wild child
not destined for prison,
but posh school instead.

I stopped for a while, years...
But now the Corporates
in their drive for profits
make mistakes.

Self-service checkouts?
This private school smile
is just waiting to take.

FACE VALUE

Before we do this thing
there are questions
I need to ask:
will you stay up with me all night,
contort your fingers, strain
your wrist, twist your tongue
until I come?

Will you pretend you haven't noticed
these piles that hang
like red dresses –
veins from hours and hours
of pushing my first-born out?
Until a locum obstetrician from Iran stepped in,
hooked my feet in stirrups
(whilst a dozen third-year students
looked on), then whisked me off
for an emergency C. section.
And two miscarriages and five more babies since,
it's a standing joke in our house
Why he didn't just put a fucking zip in.

Would you baulk at the scars
that run from hip to hip?
Naked, I look like I've been sewn together
from two different bits.
These wounds aren't yours –
not part of your past.
You weren't there
when they forced an epidural
inside my spine.
These memories aren't yours.
They're his and mine.

You might think you'll still want me
when I'm sixty-four
but will you still be wheelbarrowing
me around the kitchen floor?

And will you think your cock feels too small
with my dentures out?
'Cause I know my husband's won't –
and that's what we need to talk about.

Then there's my routine shower –
I'll get up fairly swiftly after,
wash you out. Don't be offended,
I just can't stand the stickiness
between my thighs all night.
You could have one too.
I'd like that. I would get all sleepy first
whilst you watch telly.
I wouldn't mind. I hear Newsnight
headlines as lullabies. I don't like
being left alone with the dark.
In the completeness of silence,
I am prone to be strangled
by loneliness and fear.

And I need the bedroom door
left half-ajar
so there's just a centimetre
of artificial light.
And I know this is probably obvious
but I must always sleep to your right.

And never, ever pull the duvet cover
from my naked body.
It's a long story – one I screamed about
till I almost died. To now keep locked
away in the past,
dark in my box of secrets,
waiting for someone unsuspecting
to rip their skin
on the barbed wire fence
I've tied around it

Which brings me back to this:
will you remind me to take my Prozac?
Drive me to my therapist
and back and there and back
and hold your tongue when years later
you're still picking up the tab
and I'm not getting any better?

Will you love my friends
who write poetry
and keep their own black dogs?
Will you let us meet up weekly
to discuss whose mutt is bigger and blacker
and how long it's been since we bought the collars,
owned them, named them and paraded them around –
our dark and dubious badges of honour?
Mine's more Rottweiler than Staffordshire bull terrier
though he still doesn't let go,
and we all own one
but you don't.

Would you make the mistake
of thinking you could slay my dog
or give him back
to where he came from –
was it from my parents
or my rapist ex-boyfriend?

My husband knows
because he found me, brushed me down,
held my hand to cross the road
when I was too fucked on crack
to watch my own back.
He took me home,
fed me, cleaned me,
made me whole

That reminds me:
on Tuesdays, I don't eat brown food

and if the sky's more sun than cloud
in June, I have to touch twice round every
light switch in the house.

I update my Facebook status every day
and for a *taken* woman
you might find my profile pictures
uncomfortably risqué.
You have to allow me reams of rope
but not enough to hang myself,
keep my glass half-full
but never overfill it,
remember never to agree
that my arms look fat in that
or my breasts too flat in this.

And if we ever wake at dawn,
wet and hard,
never try to kiss me
(not unless you've cleaned your teeth);
morning breath
will only ever make me retch.

I think that just about covers it.
If you still like what you see –
these perfect legs,
tight arse and expensive teeth –
and think that you can handle
all that occurs beneath,
then get stuck right in,
we can still do this thing

if I haven't gone
and put you off.

WILD THINGS

Lying with coiled springs
beneath my hips, as unfamiliar
sheets surround my skin,
I begin to text – thumbs working
overtime. Inhibitions
drowned by too many bottles
of cheap Merlot and a host who
forgot the importance of food.

'I could eat you up,
I love you so!' Send – pressed
impetuously, panic flushing
immediately. Rushing me back
home as virginal as at just
fifteen...

I must redress this revelatory
mistake. Only hours earlier,
sifting through naked salad
and beetroot falafels that stuck
like cement to my distracted
mouth, decades passing between
our last sharing of physical space,
we imparted secrets like we've been
best friends forever. Perhaps we have...

What is this game?

Too late! Formica bedside furniture
vibrates – I slide my finger across
the screen; fears allayed but
anticipation gaining its
own momentum, the message
finding a desire that mirrors my own.

Five months drift as
illicit lovers. But on the dawn of
more spiritual teachings, don't ask for
blessings through divinations.

Let me text you again, those words,
lest you fail to remember:

'I could eat you up,
I love you so!'

LESSONS FOR LOVERS OF POETS

Can we dress this up in metaphor,
wrap silk scarves of similes around us?
Perhaps leave me hanging
in drips of ellipses – maps
of erogenous zones
tracing goose bumps
like dot-to-dot colouring books;
kids' fun for adult lovers.

Tongue pushing commas –
intermission, breath for pausing,
kisses alluring me.
Alliterate me into flick, flirting,
furious, fumbling.
Keep me guessing. Please,
please, keep my interest – question
marks around my neck. Don't
let me guess. Hold
my presence with exclamation
marks skipping from my breasts.

Underline your intention
beneath my hips.
Highlight your needs
with your lips.
Acronym your pleas
inside of me.
Pinprick pupils dilate
from full stops;
calligraphy for the open-minded.
We can scribe a future
present from all of this.

Lists of others, torn
and shredded. Destroyed
as if they never existed.
Soften me with sonnets
and I will toughen you with slang.

Slip in random half-rhymes
that roll straight off your tongue...
But don't split us in half
with semi-colons,
separate beginnings too short.
Don't leave too many pauses...

Please, please finish
your sentences
as you first intended. Don't
finger-flick quotation marks
before you speak,
and if you dive in deep,
don't let go until you know
you can correction-fluid
your way back out.

Acrostic lust in
light tongue touches
Licks
Under
Silken
Thighs.
Syllable count
your foreplay
in iambic pentameter verse.
Keep the rhythm strong
but the melody light.
Leave the paraphrasing
to someone else.
And never leave sight of
how I might end up writing
this out.

LIVING THE DREAM

We were never promised the Earth
but a thousand expectations
led us to believe our
leather-bound dissertations
would hold their worth.

Between call-centre glass,
desperate mouths gasp their
share of disaffected air. Stale
body odour and sticky fingers
pick at broken packets of digestives

disintegrated on our way to work.
We dreamed of living
on our own: fast cars and women –
perhaps a mortgage, kids, a sofa purchased
on a Nationwide 'home loan'.

Twenty years of education:
a 2:1 in Sociology from Leeds...
We were never promised the Earth
but I believed – Tony's meritocracy,
aspirations to be something better

than me. Debts piling on my parents'
mantelpiece – deferment form deadlines
obligatory by June. Granny dies the moment
I find my conscience to buy stamps,
leaving me this peeling, unwanted heirloom.
Could I find a reason to stay here?
To taste salt tears of freedom,
sell surfboards barefoot in summer?
Fuck the degree, throw the debts
to the cautionary south-west wind?

Clear my lungs, hold my breath?
Smell the fear?
Live the dream?

CUSHIONING

I've never found a comfortable cushion
nor time of day;
advice, I believed, was at sunrise
or somewhere facing the open moon
of a star-struck night. An incense-ravaged
room with a candle, the obligatory
wooden Buddha placed
earnestly in the corner
struggling to breathe my mind wider,
body softer, heart stronger.

I've never found a comfortable cushion
where the edges
won't dig at the folds nor the light
burn red behind these
searching eyes. Blood thickening
around this grasping soul,
until now.

Within the domesticity of a
wilting Wednesday afternoon,
plugging the vacuum
into its socket, wires tangling around
bare feet, I drop, to my knees.
Tombstone-cold tiles beneath me,
I sit, cross-legged, hands tumbling,
eyes closing in the dimly-lit hallway
of home.

TWO LATTES

I met my friend today
for coffee;
she thinks she's dying.

I think she's hoping.

Pulling strings from the knotted
ball of wool – her life
unravelling from the inside, I try
to persuade her she should
find the words to describe
her pain.

It could be Alzheimer's,
she pretends. I nod, making the
correct gestures on the outside.
She forgets stuff, like what she
begins to say or where she
always thought she was
supposed to be going.

Then there's the pain, she explains:
vicious stabbing to the
side of her head.

Maybe CJD – the doctor said
he'll run some bloods.

I stammer to... to suggest
her life is changing, these
anomalies could be... possibly...
indicative of stress.

Silence falls between us, thickening
distance. She sips her latte with
tears in her eyes.
'Don't,' she says, grabbing my hand.
'You'll set me off.' She waves
her fingers before her face,

fanning away despair –
as if by magic, it disappears.

Everything's fine, she claims –
spooning the last
bubbles of froth
into the mouth that turns
itself back into a smile.

CONTROL CRYING

I created lives to somehow save me.
Cover cracks with Band-Aids.
Complete me or hide me
behind Mother Nature's swollen tummy,
leaking breasts, stretch marks, bio oil, nosebleeds,
kilos of Quality Street. Bleeding gums, due dates.
Kits to predict ovulation, menstruation and, at last,
a viable conception.

Morning sickness embraced – those mornings missed –
escaping into panic
of impending miscarriage. Two pink lines,
sticks of piss, repeated, continually, habitually
until a twelve-week scan confirms life
in a single flickering heartbeat.
More tests, more tests,
more tests at sixteen weeks.
One in ten thousand risk of one syndrome or another.
At thirty-six it rises, to one in two hundred and fifty.
That sounds high. The maths, of course, doesn't apply
as in your mind, the risk's been made.
What number would blind you?
And what would you do, anyway?
What ratio to decide to destroy? One in one hundred?
Fifty-fifty?
As by now you're in: belly slightly bulging, faint
internal flutterings.

There's a photo foil, like a blurred picture
of a flower processed in the fifties
and you keep it at your bedside. Not in direct sunlight
as that would fade it. And every day you trace
the outline of its face, button nose, bandy legs and pebble
toes. One spine, two ears and fingers it sucks from time to
time. One disproportionate head. Four beating chambers,
counted, measured, squared with the life you share.
A liver, two kidneys, a healthy placenta – the other end of which
attaches to every sense of inside.

So you decide, no decisions will ever be made.
Let fate deal her hand, destiny will be
the final controller of this game.

Assigned a midwife. She becomes your mother
in another life.
You open up like you've been shut forever
and she seems to like it.
One week she's absent, on a holiday or annual leave.
You feel abandoned, rejected, frustrated to explain yourself
to someone else. Like exploring the flirtations of another
faithless lover.

Birth plans: they appease your sense of self-control,
soon to discover they're barely worth the paper.
When does nature not come undone?
Your plan was never to be at home
lowing like organic cattle to please
the yoga-breathing antenatal crowd.
You wanted drugs, preferably before the labour started.
You craved sterile walls and monitors to check
the foetal heartbeat.
You got neither. The plan unravelled.
The rest's too nasty to remember. The mind does that,
else PTSD would never claim you another.

Newborns wrap you up. Not that anyone bothered
to tell you that. Well, not until you were up the duff.
It's a secret club – a Mason's handshake
only accepted when it's too damn late.
When the breasts have sagged, the nipples bleed and you
can't stop eating your own body weight in Maltesers
just to constantly feed the limpet who may as well be
still inside for all the space you get – but need.
You're so dog tired, you fall asleep
whilst changing his nappy
on your knees with the little fucker still attached,
milking you for every ounce
you've got left.

SOMETHING TROUBLES ME...

Where did all the pubes go?

I must be the only one
who didn't know
it was now in fashion
to resemble Barbie
down below.

I thought I was doing
pretty well
with my Epilady
one in May
just so spiders' legs
can't escape
through bikini Lycra

(and barely a centimetre
from the gusset).

Not naked lips
with stubble;
a fanny like a roasted duck.
Who wants that?
Transparently, I'm not as sexy
as I hoped...

Though luckily, I'm already married
else I might have to think
about giving a fuck.

PLATFORM 69

I know I'm off the rails
when I dream of men
with hooves.

And the nights are long,
drenched in sweat,
awakened by yesterday's music
still tearing through my ears.
Sleep becomes another state
of disrespect – forced
with medication
under the illusion the alternative
must be death.

Morning cup of Tetley
beneath Ikea blankets – two cats
purring, temporarily smoothing
spines of insanity.
Belly groans – no decent meal
in weeks.
Matching blood volume with
Merlot maintains my weight

just enough to keep at bay
accusations of anorexia,
infidelity and, even worse,
the cyclical disease of unadulterated
madness.
It is genetic, this lack of balance;
homeostasis as evasive as meditation
though I try, for the sake of
others, to keep these wheels
at least vaguely trailing prescriptive
expected rails.

In truth, though, this destination
is only a somewhere else
I will want to leave.

NOTHING SERIOUS

I've sustained a nasty injury, she says.
It's narcissistic –
nothing life-threatening
but fairly serious. Something I will need
to heal, should I ever not want to feel
inclined to seek out affirmation or
recognition of one kind
or another.

I wonder

how much therapy I'll need
to sort this out – or whether I can just
fuck my way through it
as I've been doing for all these years
before. It's worked for me so far.

Significantly.

Anyway, I'm unsure I can afford
another two-year course of
getting nowhere but back,
stuck brutally in a past I've
already paid to forget.

I reckon I'm exactly where
I've wanted to be: both
Mum and Dad in comfortable positions
where upon the inevitable hearing
of their death, I can sit,
protected by the supposition I
pretended all was good.

I won't be banging my fists
on their graves,
screaming procrastinated apologies
for all the terrible things I'd said.
They can rest

peacefully

believing they'd played no part
in my receiving of these
injuries.

Let's be honest! It's so fucking
clichéd to remain
blaming your parents
for your poor behaviour.
Only justifying it by paying
some over-educated cunt
forty quid an hour
to offer tissues, nod their head
and softly challenge your statements
with their bated breath.

Of course, I've never felt
'good enough' – but in these times of
meritocracy, who ever does?

Opportunity, apparently as
damaging as beauty –
one therapist said to me. Really!
And to be blessed with both?
A recipe for self-destruction
unless managed very carefully.

Oh! Poor me! Poor me!

This disappointing reality that we
must take responsibility –

that the
decisions we make
have consequences.

But if all else fails, you can still blame
your parents for your oozing set of
narcissistic injuries.

I WANT (ODE TO MY MAN/BOY)

I want a new pair of jeans but
not from that outlet GAP.
I want you to get it; I've grown out of that!
I want Dad to own a Ferrari, not a mini-bus,
and not to wind down the windows blaring
Eminem or Kanye West. And not to grope my
mum's boobs so fervently – I know he only does it
to embarrass me. I want her to wear a proper bra
when my mates come round for tea.
I want my younger brothers to fuck off and die.

I want to plug in to my iPad, count the
likes on my Instagram pictures. Find solace
in the relationship status of that fit
girl in Year Eight. I want my feet to
grow – but my penis more; definitely
before Friday night or I'll have to
stay at home. I want to write lists
of all the things I need:
mainly the top ten girls with the biggest
tits in my year. I want my clothes to be cleaned
by magic – without having to remember
to put them somewhere near the
washing machine. I can never work out
which appliance that one is.

I want my shoulders to be broader,
my voice to be much deeper, stand a
little taller. I want to move out of
bottom-set maths and into first-team
rugby. I want to choose from the
adult menu at Pizza Express and be
able to finish the Meat Feast without being sick.
I want to already know how to ollie, somersault
from the high board, I want you
to look up to me.

I want to be happy
I want to be liked.

I want to be different.
I want to fit in.
I want to do it all
without having to actually *do*
anything.
I want to find my own way.
I want to hold your hand.
I want you to tell me you love me
unconditionally, no matter what I've done.

I still need some new jeans, though, and don't judge me
for the struggle
to love my own skin.

THE LEFTOVERS

Children clinging to every limb,
squabbling over leftovers of
available skin.
Unclipped fingernails
pinch.

Sunday runners crunch
autumn's squall beneath
Nike Air Max trainers,
hot-pink Lycra reminding:

last night's glacé cherry
disaster; stale cocktails
echo in my throat. Rugby men
performing unmentionables
with matchsticks –
troubled mothers too
mashed to disguise their
morbid glancing.

Children clinging to every
limb – begging like dogs
for even negative attention.

Alcohol perforating the
pores between the
kissing gates of this
family woodland
walk.

FULL CIRCLE

I asked if we could we do it one last time –
one last time as parting lovers,
not like before when deep down
we knew there would be plenty
of other opportunities

I whispered to him, nose to nose, lips to lips,
my breath in his, 'Full circle; like a ring,
encapsulating everything –
everything missing from these scores of years.'
Pressing my breasts against his chest;
how could he not be tempted?

But, resisting, he left the room claiming
he'd be back in any minute.
Ten passed, then fifteen, as I lay strewn
in exactly the same position, arms stretched
above my head
in the way I know he loves it,
though for once, my legs crossed
in a less arrogant assumption...

There is something so beautifully addictive
in the seductive persuasion of the
meditative mind: so resolute in so many ways,
yet a dozen minutes inside of me enough to cast aside
all he knows is 'right'. Inevitably, he returned,
the divination giving blessing to all he
was about to become.
Our instincts winning for one last time.
Again.
Full circle.
The pressure's on to get it right... to leave our memory
of this night one of unity and purity.
To find the cure for the healing of these
wounds we've made.
In the beginning where he believed he could write
wrongs better and now here, back in time,

all those years ago, upon this very floor,
my hand round him –
nose to nose, lips to lips until he came.
Full circle.

Or so I claimed, but this time,
an accepting that he could be everything.
That I would not leave
still desperately lonely and ashamed. That I would not
be walking into an abusive destiny with another,
one who would torture me and later rape me –
not just of my virginity, but the core of my security,
everything that essentially
still made me child;
the one who would shape the way
I would relate to men, forever. Be so selective
about what could turn me off.
Another who, if things had been different
in this very room, perhaps
I would have never known.

Because we do change.
And bringing our pasts back to life
in the same place, years after, may sometimes
heal the seeping wounds of our mistakes.
Full circle.

And so we came together, deeply, hips to hips.
To afterwards laugh hysterically, like children,
or was it crying?
It didn't seem to matter as he went soft inside me.
There was just an understanding that whatever
had just happened, had to happen. For reasons
perhaps we would never know,
and no amount of skill or sacrifice would ever scrape
away the surface of this grief.
But now it's done and nothing could have stopped it.
Not least the ring upon my finger

or the photo of my daughter
I keep hidden in my wallet.

We lay there breathless, no guilt left in it
for either one of us. An exorcism
through our powerful embrace.
Like he always said he wanted:
a naked awareness of who we were.
And we were here:
full circle.

But it felt like there were still
unanswered questions. The first of which being:
could we ever stick to this promise
we'd so passionately made?
As he circled my lips with his tongue, I realised
we were forever tied together
on this wheel of life.

PACKING UP

Last night I packed a bag.
The first things thrown:
clean knickers, two pens,
a writing pad. Black eyeliner,
moisturiser and twenty diazepam.
The repeat prescription for
Prozac and pile cream.
The worn-in Nike Air Max, a gram
of coke, three-in-one shower gel and my
'cleanest' credit card.
If I'm going, I'm going light – but
still in plenty of style.

I don't need the car keys,
I'll be too fucked to drive. Besides,
that would be selfish; he'll need it
for the kids, their lifts, after-school
clubs and shit. Perhaps I should leave
a list... all the things to remember:

who has what in their packed
lunchbox, to take the chicken out of the
freezer on Saturday and stick in the oven
at gas mark six, for two hours,
on Sunday. The little one's
booked in at the dentist on Monday,
the cat's got his jabs and we mustn't forget
those Russell Hobbs pans
on special at Aldi.

Maybe I'll fold the washing
before I go – just quickly shove it in
the relevant cupboards. Perhaps
rustle up a casserole, so their lives
can be normal for a little while...
Actually, I'll just pick them up
from school, bring them home –
get the mother-in-law round,

then I'll go!
Okay, a quick cuddle, tell them
I'm sorry
for this morning's meltdown,
explain that it's not their fault
I struggle to cope.

Perhaps I'll have a sleep, keep
the bag packed for tomorrow –
phone a friend, have a chat about it;
these anomalies of being a wife
and mother. Open a bottle of
Merlot and hope the breaking of a
different day
brings nothing but
another poem.

TORN

If we were together, we could
share our moments between
nothing but sheets and autumn
leaves. But we won't.
Because I sit here, sipping
vodka and Diet Coke, eyed by

the gentleman at the bar – his
skin like tar and pupils wider than
his pint glass. And I need this.
You made me feel unwanted and
neurotic. There was nothing I could
think to say apart from a difficult
goodbye. I've been curbed from

writing today; 'poetry' a dirty word, a
sacrifice made for my marriage – an
abandonment of pen to paper, for
a while. Rhythms dancing waits
for me, around the corner, and
I'll love it. I'm allowed that –
providing I return, with an

appetite for sex, wet and ready.
I shall pretend to, whatever
my mind might say. Until then,
I down my drink, ice crunching
between my teeth. Tonight,
I will lose myself – and the two of you,
who tear me into parts.

One day, I will find two separate
boxes, place you both inside and
bury you. Individually, I will come
to visit you – from time to time.
Like graves.

BRITTLE BONES

She leaves like she's never been lonely,
with the bones of graves and
eyes like sensitive teeth. She speaks
with words that echo a dawn crow –
breaking through the night
silence of the unknown.

A sunset falls on the way I found her;
brittle as blackened caramel,
she snaps us into two.
My breath makes her retch
like blue cheese. She complains
I've let myself go;

complacent in my Garden of Eden,
I've helped myself to far too much.
Each word I speak feels fresh, yet
reminds her of everything she heard years ago,
as a child. Not in a good way, she adds,
like duck livers on French toast.

I loved in times when she searched
a thousand excuses for solitude –
her sour milk upon cracked lips,
hair between our fingers – so fine
it breaks upon an autumn breeze,
wisps catching across furrowed brows.

I nurtured a gratitude that flowered
with every new spring; a blooming
celebration of mutual needs. She craves
different seasons; Sahara heat or Moscow cold,
not the endless drizzle from the apologetic
skies she found.

Time is running out for catching
breaks in the weather. Her bones
tire of aching for another skin, cracking
under the weight of the forecast
she suffers. Her umbrella's broken –
though she won't tell me how.

AM I FAUSTUS?

He warned me, rearing like Mephistopheles,
of regret. And I believed him, even then,
yet powerless in my thin frame of mind
to decide otherwise. I was already on fire.
Trading my worth for infinite measures
of desire. An IOU blazoned on my back,
the rest of my life marked in scars.

It was all he gained; sitting pale in recognition
of the mistakes I was yet to make. His limbs
detaching as he morphed with grief,
the knowledge of my destination:
an eternity marked
of what will be, would be. Am I Faustus
or my truth just a distraction
as he tells himself he feels nothing?

Maybe I am the living proof that legacies
mean everything? I feel the ripples
tighten beneath my skin.

SEVENTY-THIRTY SPLIT

Twenty years on a spreadsheet,
condensed to this:
a single piece of paper you've created,
just to show me.
Tears of mine spreading hundreds into thousands –

we wish!
The reality now we've split?
Barely nothing left in the tin.
Seventy-thirty, you've been told by your solicitor
because I left you, the family home
and our kids.

What sort of mother does that make me?
Certainly not the one I dreamt of being.
That's the reality.
And we can sit, reminisce
upon times when all we wanted
was to touch and kiss

in the days when that was always enough,
just enough for each one of us.
And I do so wish,
more than anything on this Earth,
these times were here now still
attaching us.

All this poetry written,
frenetically, this past year –
for someone else to hear;
the final nail in an already
tightly squeezed coffin.

Then, that night, in our bed
whilst I lay unknowing,
soundly sleeping,
you took to reading my manuscript,
your heart bleeding with the realisation –
details of your precious wife

making love to another man, one whose name
you remembered. My cheeks brightening
when we were swapping memories
of those we had adored
from scores of years back.
Then knowing, every time
we lay in bed – together, naked
in every sense –
that I was simply waiting for the next time
I could feel his love. Not yours.
That is pain.
Pain like you could
never have known it
when twenty years ago
we took our vows; me,
I didn't believe
I was pretending
knowing the truth to be that
only time could truly tell.

And you? You, calling me destiny.
And perhaps I was.
Just not in the sense you hoped
it meant I would be.
I scan the page – no sentiment –
just either name in columns against
calculations and percentage figures.

Twenty years condensed to this.
A single Excel spreadsheet.

I break the silence and mouth my new line,
'Twenty years on a spreadsheet,'
to the Smiths' tune 'Girlfriend in a Coma'
and you say, with a wry smile,
'But that's what it's been like.'

And then the cheeks that had remained dry

begin to sparkle
with a renewed reflection of our sadness.

More silence ensues,
reminding me of all those general anaesthetics.
I laugh. Uncomfortably. And you say,
'Anything can be made sense of, on a spreadsheet.'

But to me, the lines look blurred.
So I reach out for my notepad
to print my own understanding
and desire for more and more layers
of complication.
I write these few words, instead:

Seventy-thirty split. For me,
it's always been like this.

MY DAUGHTER'S HAIR

You are right about her; I can
see it in her eyes as I begin
to leave. Through tears and the
refusal to finish her tea, she attempts
to speak of her silent pain.

I feel it too, as I lie awake
alone, pretending I can
smell her baby hair and feel her
clammy fingertips upon my
naked skin.

I have contained my fear,
disallowing this space to grieve –
refusing to hear you saying,
'She's your girl. Don't let her go.' Believing
these 'projections' not to be my truth.

Today, we will bathe together and
I will cleanse her like only her
mother can; wash and plait her locks,
clip her nails, choose sparkling tights
to match her vibrant eyes.

We will sit in windows and drink
children's 'cinos from adult glasses,
find some new slippers in the sales
to replace the cashmere ones
our puppy took to.

She can tell me over and over
about Harry and Max and how
she thinks them silly and stupid
in the playground. And I'll ask why
she thinks of them like that.

She'll laugh and try to hide her thoughts
behind her inner smile. She'll explain,
'They like to chase around and catch me.
But when they do, they pull my hair
and say they love me.'

THE BRISTOL POETRY SLAM 2015

I stand here again,
where it all began;
this very room, this spot, where
I spun my world on its axis.

A room full of strangers, bar one;
the eyes of my new lover
keeping me going
whilst I lied to my husband
who stayed at home
reading bedtime stories
to our children.

The most beautiful man
on this planet, a true man,
a bold man,
a strong man,
a kind man.

He, who acknowledged
his dark side with
intelligent management
and pride.

Whilst I stood here,
engulfed in lies,
hiding from myself,
standing proud.
Alarmingly, adoringly,
unfaithfully, mistakenly
proud of myself.

I make myself sick
to think of the photos
online: this crowd,
me, with him, sat
just over there. My hand
on his right thigh.

And I didn't care.
Not then.

Why?

I was begging
for change. Hungry
with lust. Dehydrated
from score years of marriage
where I was loved
almost too much
for my own good.
Too understood, adored
so unconditionally, I threw
my moods like toys
from a pram.

So worshipped, I believed
I had the rights of
God and the Devil
entwined.
Guilt? That never even entered
my mind.

And it was so right
I didn't win. Not then.
Not with poems
I read aloud; extended metaphors
that stretched the truth.
Rhyme schemes built
on foundations of deceit.
Similes of heaven,
the weather, skies and seas
to describe and justify
nothing more romantic
than brazen adultery.

I only ever deserved to lose.
And I lost everything.

Lost all that contained
the life I once knew:
my husband, that one
true love, my children's trust,
my self-respect, tired empathy
from others.

I don't need you to remind me
I deserve it. I already know it.
I know it every time
I wake alone, when I microwave
the meals for one, when I rely
on the headmaster's secretary
for information on my kids' behaviour.
It's a traumatic time
for them. You know?
The school makes
allowances for that.

And fuck me, this hurts.
As their lives move on with
a stepmum who surpasses
every expectation they could have
of their real one.
And my old home fills
with friends I've not seen
since the last time I stood here.

Yet I'm here again, for the second time,
a year on. Stuck in this loop –
though, this time,

alone.

THE PEN

This beautiful pen finds little ease
scratching with self-conscious narcissistic
injuries. Maybe I am too far from or
too close to my own relative luxury
to see through the flow of paper-thin
reality. Every second word the challenge
a fine line between raw emotion and banality,
persistent rhyme so useless if in my own
perverse idealism, I believe
that is all my audience wants to hear.
And do you? Does it sound good
if your delicate ears are not challenged
too much, but just enough
to keep perpetual rhythm from jarring
the simplicity? We discuss more open
spaces. Think our thoughts with clarity,
inner light, outer light, palms together
or facing out. Practise dharma to lose
our ego with every finger pointed
towards liberation.

Let me only speak for the causes
of the heartbroken masses
so in poetry slams I can hear
those clicks. Woe betide this
middle-class bitch who turned
her back on all those opportunities:
the extravagance of the red-brick
English Lit degree, not even to teach
but to indulge in how a poem
must not Mean but Be.
Running to India with a hold-all light
yet so much baggage. Fuck her, they said.
Fuck her incessant issues
when on every street corner waits
degradation to pull ugly faces
at her self-indulgent attitude.

Is it not poetic justice she struggles
to find the phrases
when words are all she came with?
Whilst within a place of dire afflictions
the wordy landscape of her hinterland
bares nothing
but exhausted clichés?

STICKS AND STONES

I've read it over and over –
each time uncovering an alternative perspective,
most of which negative, self-deprecating, blaming,
or finding chinks, flaws, an 'in' to annihilate yours.
But it's beautiful and, almost in its entirety,
the truth. But there is something missing –
as there will always be
in the outpourings of free-falling poetry.
There is only one perspective, be that of the writer
or the one who reads it.

This does not fail in helping us relate
to the torment we all face in our separate journeys
but they must never be our guide, our mantra,
our expectation:
that in others' words, we can find ourselves.
Make not the mistake of believing your life
will be richer, your relationships deeper.
One broken heart can find only its own healer.

We place our own heavy weight
upon the hearts of others.
Just as our words can lift them into open skies,
they can bury us in darkness, should we give
them the power.
St Valentine caused me pain this year
with his words, or my lack of hearing them.
I wrapped myself around
my perspective of them. Clinging
to an ideal that silence meant freedom,
that withdrawing words empowered me –
holding myself in false privacy, secret lies
to strengthen these arms
that hold you at bay. Keep my heart protected,
my pride intact. Because no one gets
the better of me...

The irony being that my complexities
control nobody else but me. Damage my own heart

far more than yours. You do not fear the bleeding,
whereas I keep plasters in my pocket –
paper-cut love
aggravating every raw nerve you touch.
But that is the way it is;
that armour we wear from childhood
rarely chink-free. And I am hurting now,
as through it, light splits
shards that pierce me.
Not paper cuts,
just open wounds requiring needle and thread.
Words can say everything but so often
absolutely nothing. And silence in its nothingness
is the most powerful communication of all.

THE MERMAID

I hear the belief in your intention, though it wasn't mine,
at least not consciously, to hold one
so out of season. We were swept,
with only the omnipresent moon
to control the tides that drowned us.
I loved you like the sea – to feel you push
and pull my mental debris;
washed-up, death-littered beaches, children poking sticks,
covering my broken pieces in rogue seaweed,
wrapped and choked,
stuffed in buckets to parade around,
their barefoot treasure to forget
on their journeys back home.

I hear the swell of your mind – a mindful effort.
No castles built on dry sand
but I wanted countless cups of castles
built with concrete.
Foundations to stand upon, flying us
like flags, proud of us.
But I could only find the quicksand.

You see, before him, I learned my speed
through quicksand; how to keep my feet
from disappearing, head above the waves,
afraid of nothing but to shut my eyes.
I tried everything until he came, lifting me
from the water's edge and
nursing me in a cave of safe protection from
the inconsistency of dangerously porous ground.

From our rock, we looked down – turbulence below,
but grateful in the knowing our anchors were tough enough
to weather the crashing sounds and rising swell.
But I still loved the sea; drawn, nakedly, its power
in just a second to wash over me, annihilate or remedy,
exhilaration conflicting with confusion
breathless as he could not make me
let the undercurrent of judgment come.

I tried walking on my hands, from my rock, to see
the sky open up differently – a sense of spinning
on the same spot. Clouds spacing birds,
tracing outlines of familiar faces, fingertips
of coral shells clinging at the water's edge.
Upside down, feet devoid of ground,
I believed in mermaids, in myths of breaths they take –
half enough to bathe on rocks, scales flipping
deep in tidal love.

So I jumped. In punishment or forgiveness
for the rock I turned to dust. Dived so deep,
I lost myself. Forever swimming against the tide.
The beach is long from sight. Salt water
loses its appeal, stings these open wounds.
Spines of slate cleave at my feet.
I am no mermaid and I should have remained
restful at my rock. I am no mermaid,
just a woman lost at sea.
I am no mermaid, I must find my feet.

HOW NOT TO SAY 'I LOVE YOU'

We do not say it like we used to:
tacked effortlessly
at the end of every phone call –
the required reassurance
after each 'goodbye', 'night-night',
'speak tomorrow'. The precursor to the expected
'I do too'. That author's note, as if we did
not already know...

You started it: left it hanging,
lying in our beds at midnight,
one hundred miles apart
Words left unspoken, agonising
in their silence.
Eight letters, three syllables,
shattering every windscreen on the M5.

My mouth hung open, lips left dry
with the muted click of communication
left to charge, closing down.
I wonder if its meaning,
the significance of sharing
those three words (sometimes only two)
so habitually and modestly, ultimately
devalues them...

Because I sometimes don't
just love you. Not in the way
of uncomplicated simplicity, in the socialised
need to be thanked, pleased or to hear
apologies. Sometimes, I fucking hate you.
Sometimes, I would love to say,
I want you, or worse, *I need you*.

To hear it just before you come
or during dinner when I catch
your eyes and they don't let go
and you say it with them,
like it is the only truth you know.

Or when I'm stoned, getting lost
in anecdotes, with giggles. And you?
You sober, wrap me up with your eyes closed
but rolling skywards, internally screaming
but kissing my hair with those three words:
'You daft cow!'

But I know what that really means
now – I know the look, the touch,
the silence...
I know behind the difficulty, challenge,
jealousy and rows, there is the
Four-Letter Word supporting,
omnipresent throughout.

Letting go of the grasping, the fear
it will not be heard, reciprocated,
used as a first-aid kit for suffering and hurt.
Let us not deface our underpinning truth
by using it like toilet paper, disposable
contact lenses or yesterday's news.
Let us keep these three words between us,
locked in our melting pot of hopes, dreams,
desires. Those Things. Those Things we keep
sacred, close, pure –
free from flippancy, overuse, insecurity and ego.

Perhaps we should never say it?
But find our unique phrase –
our own expression of what we have,
or what we want, need or lack...
Though we could just stick to the rules and
when one of us says,
'I love you,' we could leave it hanging,
like November mist, the other left wondering
what response would really be the truth.

TOPLESS

My breasts are out; pale globules
flailing at the midday sun. I can hear you
talking about them. In my head.

'Why are your nipples so long?'
Because they fed six hungry mouths.
Fuck you.
Ignorant cunt.

'They should be covered.
You must really want some.'

Want some?
More blind mishandling? Of course.
You must be right.

Did your mother deny her milk?
Are you craving your toothless fill?

Mine did their job: they swelled,
they leaked, they nourished, they bled.
They raged with fever, in tender
swollen lumps, veins like roadmaps
bursting through taut and thinning skin.

Until they shrivelled. Dried fruit.
Again and again.

Look at my hands. These fingers –
far more interesting, don't you think?
Hands that hold so many others,
soothe bitter secrets, smooth
furrowed brows. Hands that can
deliver, offer, congratulate
and pray.

Yes, my breasts are out.
Honour them like the sun.

Worship that which you fail
to understand.

Avert your stare. Hold
your silence.

They are not for you.
But you may take
these hands
instead.

THE PHONE CALL

Though the cost of this phone call
is priceless, I am splitting it
two ways, like us, down the middle –
to hear six small voices in the
sound waves we created in twenty years.
Forgive me, in this lifetime
for the crazed games
I tried so desperately
not to play. Where the expressions of my love
twisted the life we once had.
We wear our mistakes,
our selfish tendencies, like masks
for the outside world to judge.
Yet between us, in our fifty-fifty share
of blame, will come an effortless ability
to communicate clearly.

You lift the receiver.
I hear my name.
We will always soften, for one another,
the click of our open-ended
connection.

THE PHOTOGRAPH

I just saw the photograph and realised:
there'll be no more in the album
for us. Where once, linked to Facebook,
I would upload an action shot,
I am now obscured
in my new-woman home.
I guess she was there, though. Instead.

Did she catch you unawares, and snap?
Or did she solo-status her location
when you weren't around – as I once did?
And our others? Were they playing
in the sand dunes as you fixed the memory
to your iPhone – or were you too busy
looking at her? Anyway, I just wanted
to tell you: I saw the photograph,
not the one of us,
and wept.

WOTSITS

We shrink crisp packets
in the oven
and I play salt and vinegar.
Daddy, singed, heavyweight
pickled onion, sits
next to me.

A rabble of wrinkled miniatures
scatter the granite
work surface chosen when
we were something more
than shrivelled
plastic games.

You tie your replica family
together; holes through
our middles.
String spun across the ceiling
spanning the kitchen,
knots tied

to stop us slipping
too close
to one another.
Hanging like prayer flags,
fragile thread
around our delicate necks

if we dare to stand
tall enough.
We are paper dolls
with barcodes
our worth in this dance.
We dance, skipping beats

as you flick us
with your fingers.
It's that easy
within a child's mind

to free us
of our labels, to scan

the room from above
with the consciousness
of a newborn,
your eyes slit, scissors
snipping at the umbilical
cords attaching us.

SIMPLY ENOUGH

I've gained a stone since you left me.
These once-protruding bones, softened
by someone else's love. Because you did:
leave me. As I always knew you would.
Not in body; you still sat there, limbs folded,
never splayed apart.
Closed for your own protection.
Your heart, neither as open
as I once hoped. Mind overloaded,
disconnected from the spiritual information
you so tirelessly read
yet somehow always forgot to process.

I know because I felt it: I heard the words
so often as empty as the love
you thought you shared.
You plucked pieces from me
and like Robin Hood, but
disingenuously, handed them out
to all you thought might care. Yet
you never remembered to
replenish me.

But you were right, in part,
when you claimed I tried to please you.
Me! Yes, me, who for twenty years
was adored for being nothing
more special than just me.
I took 'advice' on how
to wear my hair, wore cotton
cardies to soften, covered these
angry tattoos and threw these boots
in the corner because you said
they looked too hard.
I was too hard. But you?
Rarely hard enough.
The irony, it almost
makes me smile.

I should have been quieter,
more demure, less offensive,
more spiritual, loved the environment
more – and you less. Let my hair grey
naturally but somehow still look young.
Made patience my 'thing'
and spontaneity yours
but, of course, only ever
on your terms.

Kept my needs inside myself,
not lost my temper, yet dropped
my guard. Be vulnerable. Be awake.
Be open to your journey
but never let you see me cry.

So I? I let you leave me
like this, pretending there is no fight.
And times like now,
when all I want to do is reach you,
I remind myself of how you made me feel.
You called that 'projection': my socialised
condition of ownership, lust and need.
But I've talked around this subject
and I've processed this bullshit.
In everyone else's world, mate,
it's just called reality.

So I write like this. Instead. And I write
and write and write.
And I'll write until the flesh upon these bones
begins to shine again, like it did
before I was simply not your good enough.

MEAL FOR ONE

I had a flash
of us in the aisle
at Marks', twenty years from now,
choosing citrus-
saturated duck breasts
too large for our ever-shrinking
appetites to cope with in
a single sitting. The other half
wrapped indistinguishably
in silver foil, left to rot
alongside Sunday's gelatinous lasagne
and Monday's sodden chicken pie. Why is everything always
the wrong way round?

It's a week Wednesday
on my way home
from hatha yoga, led by Jenna,
an overpriced, enthusiastic,
elastic practitioner
freshly emaciated and glassy-eyed
from her recent initiation in India.
You would laugh at her and persuade me
my best years were plentifully ahead
of me and hers, and that when she
is my age, she will kill for my cleavage
and fresh-fruit butt cheeks
you gently bit with your forever smile.

On Thursday, you chose puddings
for the weekend in tiny pots
boxed in glossy cardboard:
next week's tea light holders
once washed of lemon cheesecake
biscuit base or claustrophobic chocolate
soufflés that I would pick at,
pretending I wasn't really eating.
To twinkle any vision left in us

now, though, I use them for nothing
but buttons or the occasional ashtray.

The smoothies and the muesli
meticulously blended, weighted with
proportions of unrefined carbohydrates
and good-fat proteins, replaced now
with two cups of coffee,
double Prozac and the heavy measure
of controversy I force through
my gullet every breakfast.

FAMILY GATHERING

Cream silk frills unfold this day
the proof of demure – not least
because it is the first time here
without you at my side. Black

was expected but pale sleeves
show me well today. Short breaths,
and an undertaking of awkward
pauses; I am ill-equipped

for small talk; it causes me more
grief than even these
darkest moonless hours.
Through this great un-sleep,

I realise how easily the mind
masters tricks. I steal
another moment, maybe two,
to dance around the looking-glass,

remove accidental smudges
from beneath my eyes and to remember
how I miss your smile. Short-sighted
lenses discarded on these musty shelves

with once-used toothbrushes
and stolen hotel soap. I peel away
the cream silk frills to unfold
the rest of this wretched day

in a pair of your tracksuit bottoms
and oversized grey hoodie. You
were always so much better
at this game than me.

MISS YOU

I miss you like:
the night before Christmas
the completion of this poem
the first drag of a cigarette
the popping of a cork
the credits to my favourite film
the nightlight in my dark.
I miss you like:
the suckling of my first-born
the sip of tea at milky dawn
the beginning of a great book
the satisfaction when you come.
I miss you like:
the sand between my toes
the waves that push me under
the wind that tears my nostrils
the sun that warms my bones.
I miss you like:
there's no tomorrow
a yesterday that never was.

DEFINITION UNKNOWN

I just looked it up – to see
if it can really define me.
From the heavy Oxford version
with the broken spine and
missing sleeve, taken
twenty years ago to university
and shelved in every home I've owned.

The words I find alienate me;
portrayals of someone far beyond me,
someone I care not to know –
verbs and adjectives to make me
writhe and seethe. There is no way
on this Earth this filthy word
represents a part of me...

I always believed in life paths –
individual choices – shit happens, yet
we decide upon our own responses;
existentialism as philosophy. That was
until he came – in sweat and smells,
opinions, eyes like oceans, taking
my breath away with his smile.

I open another bottle and ponder
when I lost myself and took to
flicking through these
wafer-thin pages to remind me
of someone I care not to be.
And how many more of these
will I need
to drown these memories?

I grow so weary of these words,
close, moving on to places I would rather go:
a new life, down under? Seen the programmes,
fallen asleep to the dreams. Maybe that
would do it? Nothing there will

be the same, like opposites day –
until I realise...

I would still be saddled
with the same old mind, just upside down,
or closer to space, or without ozone –
something different but still dragging
round the original but tired brain.

The country's always been a pull.
I could take to baking apple crumble,
buy a dog, find the passion to walk,
take in the views, make idle conversation
with the few and far between neighbours
at the edge of the A road that
wrecked 'our' village years ago.

Or perhaps the sea?
The wind could whip the guilt from
within me. Draw it out in miles of
ragged coastline. I could cry
salt tears and no one
would ever know
how far I'd come...

But I know it will simply follow me,
this proverbial bad smell – no matter
where I go, or what I choose to believe.

So I rip it from the dictionary,
tear in two and shred, destroy
as if it never existed.
I doubt anyone will even notice.

How else can I solve this?
How else can I be free?
If there are no words left
to describe me,
I can wipe this slate clean.

THANKS & ACKNOWLEDGEMENTS

It is through periods like these when you discover who truly has your back! On this basis, I would like to thank those who have propped me up at the most desperate of times, those whom without, I may not have survived this past year: Simone, Emma and Barry, Hayley, Graham, Ali, Ed, Elizabeth and my wonderful sister Sue.

Lastly, but most importantly, the hugest thank you to my six beautiful, bright and inspirational children: Oscar, Alfie, Joe, Billy, Fred, Millie and my ex-husband, my first and forever love, John, whose unwavering support, even with this book, defines what it is to be unconditionally loved.

Best Intentions was published by Poetry Space (2013)

Living The Dream won the Poetry Space competition (2014)